Department of the Environment
Ancient Monuments and Historic Bui

D1335197

Maiden Castle

DORSET

SIR MORTIMER WHEELER CH, CIE, MC, TD,
D Litt, Hon V-PSA

LONDON: HER MAJESTY'S STATIONERY OFFICE

ISBN 0 11 670317 2

Contents

Maiden Castle

Recurrent features of the chalk downs of southern England, though by no means peculiar to them, are the ancient hill-top fortifications which are commonly called camps or hill forts. Neither term is wholly correct. Some of these fortifications were mere shells or refuges to which the occupants of the homesteads and villages of the countryside could have recourse in time of trouble. Others were permanently occupied as villages or small towns which fortified themselves, just as later the Romano-British or medieval valley towns fortified them-selves on the principle of self-help in an age of uncertain control. Of the latter class perhaps the most famous, though not actually the largest, is Maiden Castle, 2 miles (3km) south-west of Dorchester, in Dorset.

Excavations conducted here in 1934–37 revealed more than visitors can see today on the ground, but the superficial vestiges of this great earthwork are impressive enough. It occupies a saddle-backed hill-top, 1000yd (914m) in length, and its tumultuous three-fold defences dominate the landscape. It is thus described by Thomas Hardy: 'At one's every step forward it rises higher against the south sky, with an obtrusive personality that compels the senses to regard it and consider. The eyes may bend in another direction, but never without the con-sciousness of its heavy, high-shouldered presence at its point of vantage. . . . The profile of the whole stupendous ruin, as seen at a distance of a mile eastwards, is clearly cut as that of a marble inlay. It is varied with protuberances, which from hereabouts have the animal aspect of warts, wens, knuckles, and hips. It may indeed be likened to an enormous many-limbed organism of an antediluvian time . . . lying lifeless, and covered with a thin green cloth, which hides its substance, while revealing its contour.'

The excavations referred to showed that this imposing complex was no sudden growth. It was, in fact, the product of three distinct eras. The first era was that of the Late Stone (Neolithic) and Early Bronze Ages, roughly 3000–1500BC. After a gap of more than a thousand years, it was succeeded by the Early Iron Age and Early Roman periods, roughly 300BC to AD70, during which Maiden Castle took its present shape. A further gap ensued, and then in the fourth century AD there was a partial reoccupation which may be supposed to have dwindled to extinction in the fifth century. Thereafter, a Saxon burial of about AD600 suggests visitation rather than occupation and, save for agricultural usage, the site has remained unoccupied down to the present day. These various phases and the sub-phases with which they are diversified are briefly described in the following pages. Relics and models can be seen in the Dorset County Museum in Dorchester.

NEOLITHIC VILLAGE

The earliest Maiden Castle, if such it can be called, is no longer visible on the surface. It underlay the eastern half of the present camp, coinciding with the more easterly of the two knolls which it encompasses, and consisted of a Late Stone Age village perhaps 10 to 15 acres (4 to 6ha) in extent. The village was outlined along the marginal contour of the knoll by two lines of characteristically Neolithic flat-bottomed ditches, interrupted at frequent intervals and probably designed less as an obstacle in themselves than as quarries from which continuous embankments were derived. Axes, knives, 'scrapers' of flint, implements of bone and horn, and simple hand-made pottery of types known to archaeologists as Neolithic A—a culture here derived in all probability from Brittany—were found in considerable quantities in the ditches and in pits both within and without their perimeter. A more notable find was that of a crudely shaped chalk doll or idol (now in the Dorchester Museum), of a kind with few analogies in this country but possibly comparable with French examples and connected through them with the wide-spread cult of a Eurasiatic mother-goddess.

THE BANK-BARROW AND ITS BURIAL

This village was occupied by a pastoral and agricultural population within a measurable distance of 2000BC. It was subsequently deserted and, when we next encounter folk upon the hill-top, they are concerned with the dead rather than with the living. The funeral-monument which they left behind them is today scarcely perceptible upon the surface, but in its prime it was of astonishing magnitude. From knoll to knoll along the ridge, across the filled-up ditches of the village, a mound or bank was built between parallel trenches for a distance of no less than 587yd (537m). Actual remains of the mound have been identified for over 500ft (152m) at the eastern end, completely filling the space between the trenches, and the suggestion that the latter flanked a Neolithic racecourse like famous examples near Stonehenge and elsewhere is nullified by this fact, apart altogether from the relative narrowness of the space between the Maiden Castle trenches (only

20yd (18m) as against the 100yd (91m) width of the known Neolithic racecourses). Furthermore, not far from Maiden Castle there still exist in Long Bredy and Broadmayne parishes seemingly equivalent bank-barrows, unmutilated by Iron Age occupation and still complete with their mounds from end to end. We are compelled, therefore, to take the monstrous Maiden Castle bank-barrow at face value, and to regard it as the largest of its class but by no means without analogy.

Under the eastern end of the barrow was found a no less astonishing burial, now preserved in the Dorchester Museum as found. It was that of a man about thirty years old and about 5ft 4in (162cm) high, whose body had been hacked to pieces at and immediately after death. The skull had been slashed more than once, and the long bones had been covered with cuts, indicating thorough dismemberment prior to the careful collection and interment of the mutilated remains, some of them still in articulation.

At the time of discovery (1937) it was thought that this strange burial was contemporary with the Neolithic bank-barrow in which it occupied an axial position. Subsequent re-examination, fortified seemingly by the method of radiocarbon analysis not available until after 1949, has suggested a later date, still under discussion. Whatever the answer, the combined mutilation and apparently formal burial of the remains may be thought to imply some macabre ritual factor.

BRONZE AGE 'HIATUS'

After the Neolithic A phase, probably sometime between 2000 and 1500BC, other folk, or at least other cultures, reached the hill-top; bringers of a Neolithic B culture from northern Europe, and, a little later, of the so-called 'beakers' from the Low Countries. And then not very long after 1500BC, possibly through a climatic deterioration that rendered the high downs unattractive, the site was deserted for many centuries. Grass and scrub grew over the trenches of the bank-barrow and the shallow hollows that now represented the derelict ditches of the preceding village. A Bronze Age hunter lost his spear among the undergrowth; but it was not until the Bronze Age had long given place in north-western Europe to the Age of Iron that the ridge once more became a scene of busy life.

FIRST MAIDEN CASTLE OF THE IRON AGE

When the first users of iron reached Britain is matter of dispute, but it seems there was some infiltration during the seventh century BC, and certainly by the fourth century BC secondary Iron Age (La Tène) cultures from the Continent, particularly from north-eastern France, were familiar in the eastern and southern regions of the island. About 300BC some fresh but unidentified impetus impelled the recolonisation of the Wessex downlands and, in particular, led to the first building of Maiden Castle properly so called. By this time the downs, once more attractive to the primitive agriculturist, were beginning to fill up with farmers living partly in scattered homesteads and partly in village groups; and by one of these new village groups the site of the old

Neolithic settlement on our eastern knoll was now fortified afresh along its margins.

These third-century fortifications have been revealed by excavation beneath the main rampart of the eastern part of the present camp and under the innermost of the outworks of the eastern entrance. They are of a distinctive type inherited from the earlier part of the European Iron Age, and consist of a wall-like rampart, 9ft (2.7m) wide and 7 or 8ft (2.1 or 2.4m) high, or earth revetted front and rear by vertical timber palisades and set back some 7ft (2.1m) behind a V-shaped ditch.

9

Maiden Castle and Winterborne Monckton village from the south east in 1834; cf the description by Thomas Hardy (1840–1928) quoted on page 5. From a signed and dated watercolour by Chevalier J O C Grant

As the timbering decayed it was in part replaced externally by dry-built stone walling, of thin slabs of limestone quarried near Upwey, some 2 miles (3.2km) from the site. For its better protection, all this walling has now been buried again, as, in fact, it was already buried by those who rebuilt the camp in later pre-historic times.

Within this enclosure were timber huts, storage-pits and streets, though whether these last were originally metalled as were some of their prehistoric successors cannot now be seen, owing to the removal of the original surfaces by traffic. The huts or overground grain-stores were in some instances of rectangular or sub-rectangular plan, but the dominant method of storage for corn and other commodities was in circular pits up to 11ft (3.4m) in depth, which were sometimes, it seems, used as sumps or water-containers. How far their great numbers represent a large population and how far they are due to the constant cutting of new pits as old ones 'went sour,' cannot be assessed without far more extensive excavation than has yet been possible. As they went out of use they were deliberately filled up with debris, and thus produced much valuable evidence as to the culture of the inhabitants.

That culture was derived from the so-called 'Hallstatt' cultural complex on the Continent, with some admixture of La Tène elements. At Maiden Castle it was in a decadent or devolved condition; its pottery was for the most part of the crudest hand-made types, it had but little metalwork, and its direct contacts with the outside world were few. Corn was grown in small squarish fields such as can still be seen from the air in the vicinity, and was ground on stone slabs similar to those used by the Neolithic villagers many centuries before. Cloth was woven, and weaving-combs and massive loom-weights, mostly of chalk, are not uncommon. Brooches and other ornaments were few and may have been carefully treasured from generation to generation. The general picture is that of a self-sufficient, unenterprising peasantry.

Nevertheless, for all its simplicity, this peasantry prospered within its narrow horizons. The village was in due course extended westwards to enclose the adjacent knoll, the original western rampart being ignored or even slighted. The settlement was now some 45 acres (18ha) in extent, thrice its original size, a town rather than a village. And its entrances, east and west, were already of remarkable plan.

Even the original eastern entrance of the Iron Age village had been exceptional in the possession of two portals instead of the usual single opening. Outside these portals a considerable area had been carefully

General view from the east in 1971, showing (on the right) foundations of fourth-century Romano-British temple (see page 18) and (centre) the outline of the original western rampart and its filled-in ditch

Copyright: National Monuments Record

metalled with rammed pebbles to form a sort of *place* where wooden pens were erected, doubtless for periodical cattle markets. The entrance of the new western extension followed the pattern of the old, but both entrances were now supplemented by a projecting timber-lined hornwork (an advanced defensive work to protect an entrance through the main line of defences) which prolonged and protected their approaches, so that the town was now entered at both ends along its major axis through screened double gateways which, with the same sophisticated wall-and-berm design as that of the original defences, mark the summit of the earlier Iron Age architectural achievement in this country. Thus protected by its single rampart and ditch and its reinforced gates, the urban peasantry of Maiden Castle preserved its obstinate provincialism intact until some date in the first half of the first century BC.

LATER MAIDEN CASTLE

In order to understand what now seems to have occurred, it is necessary to cross the Channel to Brittany, and in particular to that southern part of Brittany which at the beginning of the first century BC, and doubtless earlier, was the homeland of a powerful and enterprising tribe, the Veneti. This tribe was famous for its sturdy sailing-ships, wherewith it controlled the western approaches to the Channel and carried on a vigorous trade with the Cornish peninsula. Both the Cornish and the Breton coasts bear visible vestiges of this trade in the form of identical 'cliff castles' of distinctive design, often with multiple ramparts up to three or more in number; and this expansion of the defensive system is now known to have been conditioned by the extensive use of the sling, a weapon already familiar in certain of the Mediterranean islands and particularly suited to marine warfare.

How early the sling and its antidote the multiple rampart were thus popularised in south-western Britain, we do not yet know; possibly as early as the second century BC. But by the beginning of the first century BC they were spreading to the major 'hill forts' of the interior and Maiden Castle provides a redoubtable example of this new fashion. The suggestion has been made that the innovation was encouraged by refugee chieftains from southern Brittany, where in 56BC the Veneti put up a stout resistance to Julius Caesar and were savagely punished by him; but it may well be that the remodelling of Maiden

*An ammunition dump of the first century BC: one of the hoards of
beach-pebble slingstones found in the 1934–37 excavations*

Castle had already been initiated before this episode. Early in the
first century BC for the first multiple ramparts of the site is as near a
date as the present evidence warrants.

The new model, with its slingstone background, involved a drastic
amplification of the defences. The average sling had an effective range
of something like 100yd (90m) on the level and, proportionately to the
natural slope of the ground, the defences were now multiplied to keep
the opposing slinger out of range. The remodelling shows earlier and
later phases but, in their final form as we see them today, the entrances,
where approach was naturally easiest, display a veritable cascade of
banks and ditches through which visitors deviously wind their way.
Here and there among them stone platforms, now buried, offered

vantage-points to the defenders, and the main gateways were flanked by high walls dry-built of large limestone blocks. Maiden Castle as a fortified town had reached its fullest development.

The culture associated with these multiple ramparts is characterised by pottery with a rolled or bead rim, modelled probably on metal prototypes. And its special association with the sling is represented by the large hoards of slingstones—one of them comprising as many as 20 000 selected beach-pebbles—which were deposited at this period, particularly near the gates.

EVE OF THE ROMAN INVASION

During the last few decades before the Roman invasion of AD43 certain changes occurred at Maiden Castle of a kind which suggest contact—friendly or otherwise—with the formidable Belgic settlers who, early in the first century BC, had begun to arrive in south-eastern Britain. These settlers had come from north-eastern Gaul, where Belgium preserves their name, and had been Julius Caesar's opponents during his raids on Britain in 55 and 54BC. By AD25 their influence was strong as far west as Gloucestershire; and, though there is no evidence of a Belgic conquest of Dorset, new elements in the pottery of Maiden Castle and other sites in Wessex indicate at this time a certain pervasion of Belgic ideas outside the main lines of Belgic advance. At the same period the defences of Maiden Castle were refurbished, the streets were remetalled, and the old system of underground storage was abolished, presumably in favour of barns and sheds of a less insanitary kind. The whole place, indeed, seems to have been in good order when, in AD43 or 44, it met the full shock of the Roman army. The episode was a dramatic one, and archaeology has enabled us to reconstruct it.

BATTLE AT THE EAST GATE

In the Roman scheme of conquest, the Second Augustan Legion, under the very competent command of the future emperor Vespasian, was allotted the task of subduing southern England. In the process, as his ancient biographer tells us, Vespasian reduced 'two very formidable tribes and over twenty towns, together with the Isle of Wight.' Among the twenty towns was Maiden Castle and, without detailing evidence which has been published elsewhere, the episode may be summarised as follows.

16

A casualty of the 'Battle at the East Gate,' c AD43–44: a defender's backbone pierced by a Roman arrow-head (see page 18)

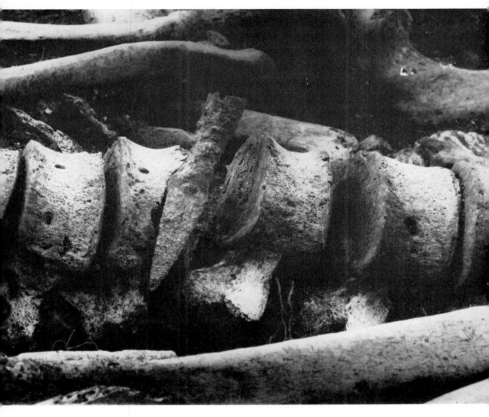

Approaching from the direction of the Isle of Wight, Vespasian's legion may be supposed to have crossed the Frome at the Dorchester crossing and to have found itself confronted, some 2 miles (3km) away, by the sevenfold ramparts of the western gates of the fortress-town, towering above the cornfields which probably swept then, as now, up to the defences. Whether any assault was attempted upon these gates we do not at present know; their excessive strength makes it more likely that Vespasian moved his main attack to the somewhat less formidable eastern end. What happened there has been revealed by excavation. First, the regiment of artillery which usually accompanied

17

a legion was ordered into action and put down a barrage of ballista-arrows. The arrows have been found about the site, and buried among the outworks was a man with an arrowhead still embedded in one of his vertebrae (to be seen in the Dorchester Museum). Following the barrage, the Roman infantry advanced up the slope, cutting its way from rampart to rampart until it reached the innermost bay, where some circular huts had recently been built. These were set alight, and under the rising clouds of smoke the gates were stormed and the position carried. But resistance had been obstinate and the fury of the legionaries was aroused. For a space, confusion and massacre dominated the scene. Men and women, young and old, were savagely cut down before the troops were called to heel. A systematic slighting of the defences followed, whereafter the legion was withdrawn, doubtless taking hostages with it, and the dazed inhabitants were left to bury their dead among the ashes of their huts beside the gates. The task was carried out anxiously and without order but, even so, from few graves were omitted those tributes of food and drink which were the proper perquisites of the dead. With their cups and food-vessels and trinkets, the bones, often two or more skeletons huddled into a single grave and many of the skulls deeply scored with sword cuts, made a sad and dramatic showing—the earliest British war-cemetery known to us.

After the battle the survivors were left in their dismantled town to continue their traditional mode of life as best they might until, with the conquest of lowland Britain and the consequent replacement of a native by a Roman economy, the new Roman town of Dorchester was ready some twenty or thirty years later to receive them. About AD70 the population finally deserted its hill-top huts and moved down into the valley, and the site of Maiden Castle reverted for a second time to pasture and tillage.

ROMANO-BRITISH TEMPLE

That was not quite the end. Although, with a brief interlude, Christianity was the official religion of the Roman Empire after AD313, it was not the only religion, and there is some evidence even for a recrudescence of a semi-Celtic paganism in Britain in the latter part of the fourth century. Certain it is that at this time, about AD380, the original (eastern) part of the old fortress became a temple-precinct, with a small temple of the square type characteristic of Celtic Gaul and Britain. Its foundations, as excavated, can still be seen, and beside them is a tiny two-roomed house for the priest, with a curiously native-looking circular hut of the same period nearby. The temple-builders adapted the ancient eastern entrance of the camp to their new purpose; one of the two portals was walled up, the other was fitted with a stone gateway and a metalled road was laid through it. West of the temple were four contemporary inhumation burials, possibly of priests who from time to time had served the god there. Who that god was we do not know. A bronze plaque from the site bears a figure of Minerva; a small bronze figurine represents a three-horned bull-god of a kind found elsewhere in Britain and in north-eastern Gaul; a fragment of a marble statuette probably represented Diana, and a Mars-like deity may also have been present. It would seem that here, as on some other native sites of the age, we are confronted with a sort of pantheon resulting from the synthetic or muddled thinking of a period when the man in the street and the farmer on the downs must alike have been puzzled often enough by the times they lived in. Near the temple lay buried a strongly built man with an iron short-sword or *scramasax* and a knife across his thigh. But by the end of the sixth century, when these bones were laid to rest, the temple must long have been a ruin; the puzzle had taken a different shape and a new pantheon had been summoned to solve it.

The substantive report on the excavations of 1934–37 was published by the Society of Antiquaries of London (1943). For Thomas Hardy's burlesque account of an older excavation, see 'A Tryst in an Ancient Earthwork,' included in 'A Changed Man . . . and Other Tales' (1913).
The site was placed in the guardianship of the Commissioners of HM Works in 1908 by Lord Alington. In 1913 it became the property of the Duchy of Cornwall.

Printed in Scotland by Her Majesty's Stationery Office at HMSO Press, Edinburgh
Dd 0697713 K94 4/80 (17090)